BASIC BIOGRAPHIES

# Albert Einstein

by Susan Kesselring

$$E = mc^2$$

Albert Einstein loved **science**. He was very smart. His ideas changed science in many ways.

Albert Einstein had many new ideas about science.

3

Albert was born in Germany on March 14, 1879. He did not talk much when he was little. But he was always thinking.

Albert had a sister, Maja (left). Albert was eight years old in this photo.

When Albert was five, he got a **compass** from his dad. He liked it. The compass made Albert want to learn more about science.

By the 1920s, Albert was a **scientist**.

Albert went to school. It was hard for him. Albert liked thinking and learning on his own much better.

Even at age 40, Albert learned better on his own.

Albert grew up. He started to think about time, space, and **energy**. He had new ideas about these things. Albert's ideas had never been thought of before.

Albert learned new things about time, space, and energy.

Albert wrote papers about his new ideas. He also worked as a teacher. Now other people could think about Albert's ideas, too.

Albert shared his ideas with other people.

Albert's ideas helped people **invent** new things. They invented TVs, cameras, and **lasers**. Soon, Albert won a prize for his ideas about science.

Albert met these scientists in 1931.

Albert also wanted peace in the world. He did not like war. He told people about these ideas, too.

One of Albert's hobbies was sailing.

In 1933, Albert moved to the United States. He lived there for the rest of his life.

Albert became a U.S. citizen in 1940.

Albert died in 1955. His new ideas about science had changed the world.

Albert's ideas changed the world.

# Glossary

**compass (KUM-puss):** A compass is a tool that shows north, south, east, and west. People use compasses to tell direction.

**energy (EN-ur-jee):** Energy is the power to do work. It takes energy to move things and to make things hot.

**invent (in-VENT):** To invent is to come up with an idea and make something new. Someone used Albert's ideas to invent lasers.

**lasers (LAY-zur):** A laser is a thin, strong beam of light. Some lasers are strong enough to cut things.

**science (SYE-unss):** Science is the study of nature and the world. Albert had new ideas about science.

**scientist (SYE-uhn-tist):** A scientist is a person who studies the world by testing, experimenting, and measuring. Albert was a scientist.

# To Find Out More

## Books

Brown, Don. *Odd Boy Out: Young Albert Einstein.* New York: Houghton Mifflin Company, 2004.

Lakin, Patricia. *Albert Einstein: Genius of the Twentieth Century.* New York: Aladdin, 2005.

Wishinsky, Frieda. *What's the Matter With Albert?: A Story of Albert Einstein.* Toronto, Ontario: Maple Tree Press, 2002.

## Web Sites

Visit our Web site for links about Albert Einstein: *childsworld.com/links*

Note to Parents, Teachers, and Librarians: We routinely verify our Web links to make sure they are safe and active sites. So encourage your readers to check them out!

# Index

# About the Author

**Susan Kesselring** has taught all ages of children from preschool through grade 8. She has been a certified Reading Recovery teacher and director of a preschool. She loves to help children get excited about learning. Family, friends, books, music, and her dog, Lois Lane, are some of her favorite things.

**On the cover: Albert Einstein writes his ideas on a chalkboard.**

Published by The Child's World®
1980 Lookout Drive • Mankato, MN 56003-1705
800-599-READ • www.childsworld.com

ACKNOWLEDGMENTS
The Child's World®: Mary Berendes, Publishing Director
The Design Lab: Design and production
Red Line Editorial: Editorial direction

PHOTO CREDITS: AP Images, cover, 7, 9, 11, 13, 15, 17, 21; Mark Aplet/
iStockphoto, cover, 1, 10, 22; STR/AP Images, 3; Hulton Archive/
Stringer/Getty Images, 5; Library of Congress, 19

Printed in the United States of America in Mankato, Minnesota.
November 2009
F11460

LIBRARY OF CONGRESS CATALOGING-IN-PUBLICATION DATA
Kesselring, Susan.
  Albert Einstein / by Susan Kesselring.
    p. cm. — (Basic biographies)
  Includes index.
  ISBN 978-1-60253-338-7 (lib. bdg. : alk. paper)
  1. Einstein, Albert, 1879-1955—Juvenile literature. 2. Physicists—Biography—Juvenile literature. I. Title. II. Series.
  QC16.E5K47 2010
  530.092—dc22 [B]                                                    2009029363